MY FIRST SPORTS

Snowboarding

by Ray McClellan

I0890187

BLASTOFF! READERS 4

BELLWETHER MEDIA • MINNEAPOLIS, MN

Note to Librarians, Teachers, and Parents:

Blastoff! Readers are carefully developed by literacy experts and combine standards-based content with developmentally appropriate text.

Level 1 provides the most support through repetition of high-frequency words, light text, predictable sentence patterns, and strong visual support.

Level 2 offers early readers a bit more challenge through varied simple sentences, increased text load, and less repetition of high-frequency words.

Level 3 advances early-fluent readers toward fluency through increased text and concept load, less reliance on visuals, longer sentences, and more literary language.

Level 4 builds reading stamina by providing more text per page, increased use of punctuation, greater variation in sentence patterns, and increasingly challenging vocabulary.

Level 5 encourages children to move from "learning to read" to "reading to learn" by providing even more text, varied writing styles, and less familiar topics.

Whichever book is right for your reader, Blastoff! Readers are the perfect books to build confidence and encourage a love of reading that will last a lifetime!

This edition first published in 2011 by Bellwether Media, Inc.

No part of this publication may be reproduced in whole or in part without written permission of the publisher. For information regarding permission, write to Bellwether Media, Inc., Attention: Permissions Department, 5357 Penn Avenue South, Minneapolis, MN 55419.

Library of Congress Cataloging-in-Publication Data
McClellan, Ray.
Snowboarding / by Ray McClellan.
p. cm. – (Blastoff! readers: My first sports)
Includes bibliographical references and index.
Summary: "Simple text and full-color photography introduce beginning readers to the sport of snowboarding. Developed by literacy experts for students in grades two through five"–Provided by publisher.
ISBN 978-1-60014-463-9 (hardcover : alk. paper)
1. Snowboarding–Juvenile literature. I. Title.
GV857.S57M3635 2010
796.939–dc22 2010000809

Text copyright © 2011 by Bellwether Media, Inc. BLASTOFF! READERS and associated logos are trademarks and/or registered trademarks of Bellwether Media, Inc.

Printed in the United States of America, North Mankato, MN.
080110 1162

Contents

What Is Snowboarding? 4

The Basic Rules of Snowboarding 8

Snowboarding Equipment 14

Snowboarding Today 18

Glossary 22

To Learn More 23

Index 24

What Is Snowboarding?

Snowboarding is a sport where people use snowboards to ride down snow-covered slopes. An early version of snowboarding began in the 1960s. Sherman Poppen made a toy he called a **Snurfer** for his daughter. It was for surfing on the snow.

The first modern snowboards were made in the 1970s. More and more people tried to **carve** down slopes on snowboards. Some people started using **ramps** to do jumps and tricks.

The first **Winter X Games** in 1997 helped make the sport more popular. Snowboarding became part of the **Winter Olympics** in 1998.

The Basic Rules of Snowboarding

There are many kinds of snowboarding events. The **half-pipe** is the most popular. Boarders ride down a long half-pipe.

They jump and do tricks as they ride back and forth. Judges score them based on how hard their tricks are and how well they perform them.

fun fact

The largest half-pipes are called super-pipes. Boarders can get the most air from super-pipes.

In **slopestyle** events, boarders ride down a slope that has jumps, bumps, and rails. Each rider chooses their own path down the slope. Judges score riders based on the tricks they do.

In **Big Air** contests, boarders jump off a huge ramp. Judges score them on the height of their jumps and the tricks they do in the air.

fun fact

In Super G, boarders can reach speeds up to 45 miles (72 kilometers) per hour.

Racing is also popular. In **slalom** events, boarders race through sets of gates. In **Super G**, boarders cruise down steep slopes at top speeds. Boarders go one at a time in these races. The rider with the fastest time wins.

In **boardercross**, four boarders start at the top of a course at the same time. They bump and pass each other on a course of curves and jumps. The first to cross the finish line wins.

Snowboarding Equipment

Every boarder needs a good snowboard. Most boards are made of wood and **carbon fiber**.

fun fact

"Flex" measures a board's flexibility. Soft boards are very flexible for doing tricks. Hard boards have less flex, but they are better for turning and racing.

Racing boards are long and narrow. Boards for doing tricks are shorter and wider.

Boarders also need **bindings**, boots, helmets, and warm clothes. Bindings connect the boots to the board.

A helmet protects a boarder's head during falls. Some boarders also wear wrist, elbow, and knee pads for extra protection.

Snowboarding Today

Snowboarding is popular wherever there are snow-covered slopes. Most ski hills and resorts have areas for snowboarding. Some boarders just like cruising down a slope. Others head for a half-pipe and try to pull off flips, spins, **grabs**, and other tricks.

Torah Bright

The best snowboarders can become **professionals**. They compete in tournaments around the world for cash prizes.

Shaun White

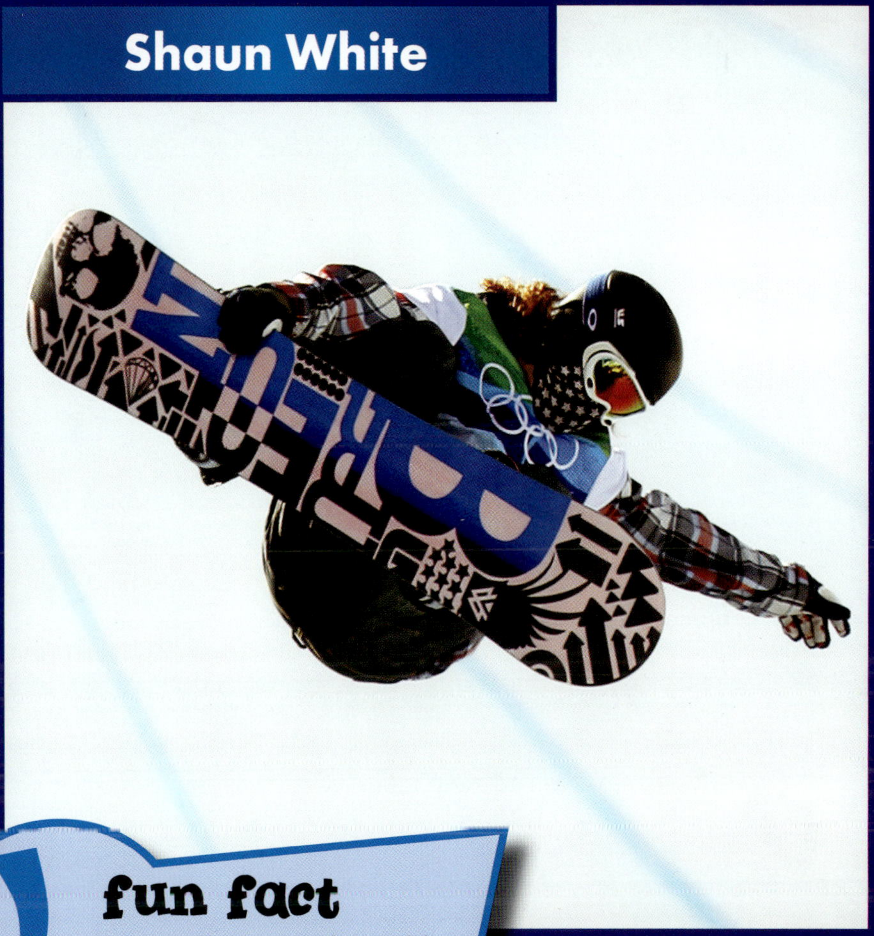

fun fact

Shaun White won the gold medal in the half-pipe event at the 2010 Winter Olympics.

Fans love to watch stars like Shaun White, Travis Rice, and Torah Bright pull off huge tricks. Do you think you could carve the slopes like they do?

Glossary

Big Air—a snowboarding event in which boarders do high jumps and tricks off of a huge ramp

bindings—the equipment that connects a boarder's boots to the board

boardercross—a snowboarding race in which four boarders start a course together, bumping and passing each other in a race to the finish line

carbon fiber—a strong, lightweight material made from very thin strands of carbon woven together

carve—to go down a hill on a snowboard while turning slightly on one edge of the board

grabs—tricks in which a snowboarder grabs part of the board while in the air

half-pipe—a type of ramp that is shaped like a "U"

professionals—people who are paid to play a sport

ramps—inclines that snowboarders jump off to do tricks

slalom—a type of downhill race in which racers must weave between a series of gates

slopestyle—a type of snowboarding event in which boarders do tricks as they go down a slope covered with obstacles

Snurfer—an early version of the snowboard, first introduced in the 1960s

Super G—a snowboarding race in which boarders speed down a steep slope, reaching tremendous speeds

Winter Olympics—a worldwide sporting event held every four years

Winter X Games—a popular competition for a wide range of winter action sports, including snowboarding

To Learn More

AT THE LIBRARY

Endres, Hollie J. *Snowboarding*. Minneapolis, Minn.: Bellwether Media, 2008.

Fitzpatrick, Jim. *Snowboarding*. Ann Arbor, Mich.: Cherry Lake Publishing, 2008.

Gustaitis, Joseph. *Snowboard*. New York, N.Y.: Crabtree Publishing, 2009.

ON THE WEB

Learning more about snowboarding is as easy as 1, 2, 3.

1. Go to www.factsurfer.com.
2. Enter "snowboarding" into the search box.
3. Click the "Surf" button and you will see a list of related Web sites.

With factsurfer.com, finding more information is just a click away.

Index

1960s, 5
1970s, 6
1997, 7
1998, 7
2010, 21
Big Air, 11
bindings, 16
boardercross, 13
boots, 16
Bright, Torah, 20, 21
carbon fiber, 14
carving, 6, 21
flex, 15
flips, 19
grabs, 19
half-pipe, 9, 19, 21
helmet, 16, 17
judges, 9, 10, 11
Poppen, Sherman, 5
professionals, 20
rails, 10
ramps, 6, 11
Rice, Travis, 21
slalom, 12
slopestyle, 10
snowboards, 5, 6, 14, 15, 16
Snurfer, 5
spins, 19
Super G, 12
super-pipe, 9
tricks, 6, 9, 10, 11, 15, 19, 21
White, Shaun, 21
Winter Olympics, 7, 21
Winter X Games, 7

The images in this book are reproduced through the courtesy of: Kevin Arnold/Getty Images, front cover, pp. 10, 18-19; waldhaeusel.com/Age Fotostock, pp. 4-5; Bruce McGowan/Alamy, p. 6; David Zalubowski/AP Images, p. 7; Natalie Jean, pp. 8-9; Postnikova Kristina, p. 11; WireImage/Getty Images, pp. 12, 20; Sports Illustrated/Getty Images, p. 13; Juan Martinez, pp. 14-15, 19 (small); Larry Prosor/Photolibrary, p. 16; Adie Bush/Photolibrary, p. 17; Cameron Spencer/Getty Images, p. 21.